MW00875597

The F.L.Y.

FEARLESSLY LOVE YOURSELF

Journal

BY TRINA NICOLE

COPYRIGHT © 2021 CATRINA CLAYTON COMMUNICATIONS LLC

ALL RIGHTS RESERVED.

REPRODUCTION OF TEXT IN PART OR WHOLE WITHOUT THE EXPRESS WRITTEN CONSENT BY THE AUTHOR IS NOT PERMITTED AND IS UNLAWFUL ACCORDING TO THE 1976 UNITED STATES COPYRIGHT ACT.

www.flygirlwithfibro.com

Hey Fly Girl!

I'M SO HAPPY YOU DECIDED TO GET THE F.L.Y. JOURNAL! I'VE BEEN ON MY OWN HEALING JOURNEY FOR A FEW YEARS AND MY MISSION HAS ALWAYS BEEN TO HELP OTHERS ALONG THEIR JOURNEY BY SHARING MY STORY & EXPERIENCES.

AFTER DEALING WITH MY OWN FEELINGS OF SELF-DOUBT, QUESTIONING MY VALUE & WORTH, NOT FULLY FLOWING IN MY SELF-LOVE, I STARTED TO JOURNAL.

I WAS LOOKING FOR MORE WAYS TO ENGAGE IN MY SELF-LOVE & SELF-CARE BUT COULDN'T FIND EXACTLY WHAT I WAS LOOKING FOR, SO I DECIDED TO CREATE WHAT I WANTED.

THIS JOURNAL IS A TOOL TO HELP YOU ENGAGE IN DAILY SELF-LOVE & SELF-CARE. EACH DAYS STARTS WITH AN AFFIRMATION (TO SAY), AN ACTIVITY (TO DO) AND A JOURNAL PROMPT (TO WRITE).

THE "SLAYED THE DAY" PAGE ALLOWS YOU TO CHECK-IN WITH YOURSELF AND HOW YOUR DAY WENT. BY REFLECTING ON THE DAY, YOU CAN NOTICE PATTERNS, TRIGGERS, OR EVEN HOW YOUR MOOD FLUCTUATED DEPENDING ON WHAT YOU DID THAT DAY. SELF-AWARENESS COMES BEFORE THE LEAP FORWARD INTO PERSONAL TRANSFORMATION.

REMEMBER, SELF-LOVE IS ENTIRELY UP TO YOU! AFFIRM YOURSELF AND WHAT YOU WANT FOR YOUR LIFE. BELIEVE IT IS ALREADY YOURS. BELIEVE YOU DESERVE IT, BECAUSE YOU DO! **IT'S TIME FOR YOU TO F.L.Y., "FEARLESSLY LOVE YOURSELF" INTO THE LIFE YOU DESERVE.**

XOXO,

Trina Nicole

SELF-LOVE IS THE BEST LOVE.

"I am Bold and Beautiful

Sis, put on your favorite lipstick, take a cute selfie & remind yourself of how fly you are!

WRITE A DESCRIPTION OF YOURSELF USING ONLY LOVING WORDS.

_____

_____

_____

_____

_____

_____

_____

_____

Slayed the Day

TODAY, I'M GRATEFUL FOR: _____

WHAT I ATE TODAY:

Breakfast: _____

Snacks: _____

Lunch: _____

Dinner: _____

HOW MANY OZ. OF WATER I DRANK:

HOW MANY MINS. OF EXERCISE/ MEDITATION I DID :

DAILY REFLECTION:

_____

_____

_____

HOW MANY HOURS OF SLEEP I GOT LAST NIGHT:

HOW MANY HOURS OF SLEEP I PLAN TO GET TONIGHT:

My Thoughts

YOU ARE THE DIVINE DESIGNER OF YOUR LIFE.

Girl, go buy yourself some pretty flowers.

LIST 3 THINGS YOU LOVE ABOUT YOURSELF.

_____

_____

_____

_____

_____

_____

_____

_____

Slayed the Day

TODAY, I'M GRATEFUL FOR: _____

WHAT I ATE TODAY:

Breakfast: _____

Snacks: _____

Lunch: _____

Dinner:

HOW MANY OZ. OF WATER I DRANK:

HOW MANY MINS. OF EXERCISE/ MEDITATION I DID :

DAILY REFLECTION:

_____

_____

_____

HOW MANY HOURS OF SLEEP I GOT LAST NIGHT:

HOW MANY HOURS OF SLEEP I PLAN TO GET TONIGHT:

My Thoughts

THERE IS NO DEADLINE FOR HEALING YOUR HEART.

"I am water. I cry, I cleanse, I flow"

Queen, light some candles and take a long, hot bath.

WHAT IN YOUR LIFE IS DRAINING YOUR ENERGY & HOW CAN YOU CHANGE IT?

_____

_____

_____

_____

_____

_____

_____

_____

Slayed the Day

TODAY, I'M GRATEFUL FOR: _____

WHAT I ATE TODAY:

Breakfast: _____

Snacks: _____

Lunch: _____

Dinner: _____

HOW MANY OZ. OF WATER I DRANK:

HOW MANY MINS. OF EXERCISE/ MEDITATION I DID :

DAILY REFLECTION:

_____

_____

_____

HOW MANY HOURS OF SLEEP I GOT LAST NIGHT:

HOW MANY HOURS OF SLEEP I PLAN TO GET TONIGHT:

My Thoughts

LISTEN TO YOUR INTUITION & LET IT GUIDE YOU.

"I am not hurting, I am healing"

Sis, meditate.
Sit still and be quiet for at least
10 minutes today.

WHAT PAIN AND ANGER ARE YOU HOLDING ONTO AND HOW CAN YOU LET IT GO?

_____

_____

_____

_____

_____

_____

_____

_____

TODAY, I'M GRATEFUL FOR: _____

WHAT I ATE TODAY:

Breakfast: _____

Snacks: _____

Lunch: _____

Dinner:

HOW MANY OZ. OF WATER I DRANK:

HOW MANY MINS. OF EXERCISE/ MEDITATION I DID :

DAILY REFLECTION:

_____

_____

_____

HOW MANY HOURS OF SLEEP I GOT LAST NIGHT:

HOW MANY HOURS OF SLEEP I PLAN TO GET TONIGHT:

My Thoughts

YOU ARE BEAUTIFUL INSIDE & OUT.

I am in the midst of transformation

Babe, treat yourself
to a mani/pedi.

WHAT IS SOMETHING YOU WANT TO DO BUT HAVE BEEN TO AFRAID TO TRY?

_____

_____

_____

_____

_____

_____

_____

_____

Slayed the Day

TODAY, I'M GRATEFUL FOR: _____

WHAT I ATE TODAY:

Breakfast:
Snacks:
Lunch:
Dinner:

HOW MANY OZ. OF WATER I DRANK:

HOW MANY MINS. OF EXERCISE/ MEDITATION I DID :

DAILY REFLECTION:

HOW MANY HOURS OF SLEEP I GOT LAST NIGHT:

HOW MANY HOURS OF SLEEP I PLAN TO GET TONIGHT:

My Thoughts

STAY TRUE TO YOURSELF, ALWAYS.

> *"I radiate love and others reflect love back to me"*

Girl, Namaste & Slay.
Take a yoga class or practice it at home.

HOW CAN YOU SET BETTER BOUNDARIES IN YOUR LIFE?

_____

_____

_____

_____

_____

_____

_____

_____

Slayed the Day

TODAY, I'M GRATEFUL FOR: _____

WHAT I ATE TODAY:

Breakfast: _____

Snacks: _____

Lunch: _____

Dinner:

HOW MANY OZ. OF WATER I DRANK:

HOW MANY MINS. OF EXERCISE/ MEDITATION I DID :

DAILY REFLECTION:

_____

_____

_____

HOW MANY HOURS OF SLEEP I GOT LAST NIGHT:

HOW MANY HOURS OF SLEEP I PLAN TO GET TONIGHT:

My Thoughts

DEFINE YOUR OWN DESTINY.

"I am my thoughts, my thoughts are me"

Queen, it's time to relax. Pamper yourself with a massage.

WHAT CAN YOU CHANGE IN YOUR LIFE TO MAKE ROOM FOR MORE HAPPINESS?

_____

_____

_____

_____

_____

_____

_____

_____

Slayed the Day

TODAY, I'M GRATEFUL FOR: _____

WHAT I ATE TODAY:

Breakfast: _____

Snacks: _____

Lunch: _____

Dinner: _____

HOW MANY OZ. OF WATER I DRANK: [ ]

HOW MANY MINS. OF EXERCISE/ MEDITATION I DID : [ ]

DAILY REFLECTION:

_____

_____

_____

HOW MANY HOURS OF SLEEP I GOT LAST NIGHT: [ ]

HOW MANY HOURS OF SLEEP I PLAN TO GET TONIGHT: [ ]

My Thoughts

BE THE ONE IN CONTROL OF YOUR LIFE.

> *"I am grateful for the life force energy that flows through me"*

Babe, just dance!
Put on some music and
dance like nobody is watching!

WHAT IS GOING WELL FOR YOU IN YOUR LIFE RIGHT NOW?

_____

_____

_____

_____

_____

_____

_____

_____

Slayed the Day

TODAY, I'M GRATEFUL FOR: _____

WHAT I ATE TODAY:

Breakfast:	
Snacks:	
Lunch:	
Dinner:	

HOW MANY OZ. OF WATER I DRANK:

HOW MANY MINS. OF EXERCISE/ MEDITATION I DID :

DAILY REFLECTION:

_____
_____
_____

HOW MANY HOURS OF SLEEP I GOT LAST NIGHT:

HOW MANY HOURS OF SLEEP I PLAN TO GET TONIGHT:

My Thoughts

YOU MATTER & YOU ARE ENOUGH.

> *"I will not be stuck in my past, I look forward to my future*

Sis, it's time to unplug.
Stay off social media for one day.

NAME 3 THINGS OTHERS WOULD SAY YOU'RE AN EXPERT AT.

_____

_____

_____

_____

_____

_____

_____

Slayed the Day

TODAY, I'M GRATEFUL FOR: _____

WHAT I ATE TODAY:

Breakfast: _____

Snacks: _____

Lunch: _____

Dinner:

HOW MANY OZ. OF WATER I DRANK:

HOW MANY MINS. OF EXERCISE/ MEDITATION I DID :

DAILY REFLECTION:

HOW MANY HOURS OF SLEEP I GOT LAST NIGHT:

HOW MANY HOURS OF SLEEP I PLAN TO GET TONIGHT:

My Thoughts

YOU ARE PRETTY & POWERFUL.

"I will not hold hate in my heart"

Spread the love, Girl!
Do something nice for
someone else today.

WHAT'S ONE CHOICE YOU CAN MAKE RIGHT NOW THAT YOUR FUTURE SELF WILL THANK YOU FOR?

_____

_____

_____

_____

_____

_____

_____

_____

Slayed the Day

TODAY, I'M GRATEFUL FOR: _____

WHAT I ATE TODAY:

Breakfast: _____

Snacks: _____

Lunch: _____

Dinner: _____

HOW MANY OZ. OF WATER I DRANK:

HOW MANY MINS. OF EXERCISE/ MEDITATION I DID :

DAILY REFLECTION:

_____

_____

_____

HOW MANY HOURS OF SLEEP I GOT LAST NIGHT:

HOW MANY HOURS OF SLEEP I PLAN TO GET TONIGHT:

My Thoughts

YOU
ARE
MAGICAL.

"My body is healthy & my mind is brilliant"

You are what you eat, Babe!
Eat a healthy lunch,
no fast food or soda today!

WHAT DO YOU NEED TO FORGIVE YOURSELF FOR?

_____

_____

_____

_____

_____

_____

_____

_____

Slayed the Day

TODAY, I'M GRATEFUL FOR: _____

WHAT I ATE TODAY:

Breakfast: _____

Snacks: _____

Lunch: _____

Dinner: _____

HOW MANY OZ. OF WATER I DRANK:

HOW MANY MINS. OF EXERCISE/ MEDITATION I DID :

DAILY REFLECTION:

_____

_____

_____

HOW MANY HOURS OF SLEEP I GOT LAST NIGHT:

HOW MANY HOURS OF SLEEP I PLAN TO GET TONIGHT:

My Thoughts

DON'T LET ANYTHING STOP YOU FROM MAKING IT HAPPEN.

"Creative energy flows through me and leads me to new ideas"

Tap into your creativity, Queen!
Spend some time creating, painting, drawing, or even writing.

WHAT IN YOUR LIFE IS DRAINING YOUR ENERGY RIGHT NOW? HOW CAN YOU CHANGE IT?

_____

_____

_____

_____

_____

_____

_____

_____

Slayed the Day

TODAY, I'M GRATEFUL FOR: _____

WHAT I ATE TODAY:

Breakfast:
Snacks:
Lunch:
Dinner:

HOW MANY OZ. OF WATER I DRANK:

HOW MANY MINS. OF EXERCISE/ MEDITATION I DID :

DAILY REFLECTION:

HOW MANY HOURS OF SLEEP I GOT LAST NIGHT:

HOW MANY HOURS OF SLEEP I PLAN TO GET TONIGHT:

My Thoughts

YOU DESERVE LOVE, SUCCESS, & HAPPINESS IN YOUR LIFE.

Babe, alone time is necessary!
Take yourself on a date.

WHAT THINGS ARE YOU GRATEFUL FOR IN YOUR LIFE?

_____

_____

_____

_____

_____

_____

_____

_____

Slayed the Day

TODAY, I'M GRATEFUL FOR: _____

WHAT I ATE TODAY:

Breakfast:
Snacks:
Lunch:
Dinner:

HOW MANY OZ. OF WATER I DRANK:

HOW MANY MINS. OF EXERCISE/ MEDITATION I DID :

DAILY REFLECTION:

HOW MANY HOURS OF SLEEP I GOT LAST NIGHT:

HOW MANY HOURS OF SLEEP I PLAN TO GET TONIGHT:

My Thoughts

PROTECT YOUR PEACE.

"I have been given endless talents that I will utilize"

Girl, it's time to get rid of stuff!
Clean and declutter a space today.

WHAT'S SOMETHING NEGATIVE THAT YOU NEED TO GET RID OF?

_____

_____

_____

_____

_____

_____

_____

_____

Slayed the Day

TODAY, I'M GRATEFUL FOR: _____

WHAT I ATE TODAY:

Breakfast:
Snacks:
Lunch:
Dinner:

HOW MANY OZ. OF WATER I DRANK:

HOW MANY MINS. OF EXERCISE/ MEDITATION I DID :

DAILY REFLECTION:

HOW MANY HOURS OF SLEEP I GOT LAST NIGHT:

HOW MANY HOURS OF SLEEP I PLAN TO GET TONIGHT:

My Thoughts

YOU CAN'T SAVE EVERYBODY. SAVE YOURSELF FIRST.

"I abandon my old habits & take up new, positive ones

Sis, be one with nature.
Spend some time outside, take in the fresh air and stop to smell the roses.

WHAT ARE YOUR BAD HABITS & HOW CAN YOU STOP DOING THEM?

_____

_____

_____

_____

_____

_____

_____

_____

Slayed the Day

TODAY, I'M GRATEFUL FOR: _____

WHAT I ATE TODAY:

Breakfast:
_____

Snacks:
_____

Lunch:
_____

Dinner:

HOW MANY OZ. OF WATER I DRANK:

HOW MANY MINS. OF EXERCISE/ MEDITATION I DID :

DAILY REFLECTION:

_____
_____
_____

HOW MANY HOURS OF SLEEP I GOT LAST NIGHT:

HOW MANY HOURS OF SLEEP I PLAN TO GET TONIGHT:

My Thoughts

KNOW YOUR WORTH & EXACTLY WHAT YOU DESERVE.

"My ability to conquer challenges is limitless"

Queen, sleep is everything! Commit to going to bed earlier and getting a full night's rest.

WHAT DO YOU NEED TO START SAYING "YES" TO?

Slayed the Day

TODAY, I'M GRATEFUL FOR: _____

WHAT I ATE TODAY:

Breakfast:
Snacks:
Lunch:
Dinner:

HOW MANY OZ. OF WATER I DRANK:

HOW MANY MINS. OF EXERCISE/ MEDITATION I DID :

DAILY REFLECTION:

HOW MANY HOURS OF SLEEP I GOT LAST NIGHT:

HOW MANY HOURS OF SLEEP I PLAN TO GET TONIGHT:

My Thoughts

GIRL, TWIRL ON YOUR HATERS.

"My body is a temple and I honor it"

Sis, health is wealth!
Try a new recipe and cook a healthy dinner.

WHAT ARE YOUR BIGGEST HOPES & DREAMS FOR YOUR LIFE?

_____

_____

_____

_____

_____

_____

_____

_____

Slayed the Day

TODAY, I'M GRATEFUL FOR: _____

WHAT I ATE TODAY:

Breakfast: _____

Snacks: _____

Lunch: _____

Dinner: _____

HOW MANY OZ. OF WATER I DRANK:

HOW MANY MINS. OF EXERCISE/ MEDITATION I DID :

DAILY REFLECTION:

_____

_____

_____

HOW MANY HOURS OF SLEEP I GOT LAST NIGHT:

HOW MANY HOURS OF SLEEP I PLAN TO GET TONIGHT:

My Thoughts

ALWAYS SHOW UP AS YOUR TRUE, AUTHENTIC SELF.

Queen, laughter is good for the soul!
Watch your favorite funny movie
or tv show.

WHAT MAKES YOU HAPPY ?

_____

_____

_____

_____

_____

_____

_____

_____

Slayed the Day

TODAY, I'M GRATEFUL FOR: _____

WHAT I ATE TODAY:

Breakfast: _____

Snacks: _____

Lunch: _____

Dinner:

HOW MANY OZ. OF WATER I DRANK:

HOW MANY MINS. OF EXERCISE/ MEDITATION I DID :

DAILY REFLECTION:

HOW MANY HOURS OF SLEEP I GOT LAST NIGHT:

HOW MANY HOURS OF SLEEP I PLAN TO GET TONIGHT:

My Thoughts

YOU FACE GREAT OBSTACLES BECAUSE THERE IS GREATNESS IN YOU.

I will not apologize for being myself

Babe, when you look good, you feel good!
Put on your favorite outfit and make sure to
add some cute accessories!

WHAT IS YOUR FAVORITE BODY PART & WHY?

Slayed the Day

TODAY, I'M GRATEFUL FOR: _____

WHAT I ATE TODAY:

Breakfast:
Snacks:
Lunch:
Dinner:

HOW MANY OZ. OF WATER I DRANK:

HOW MANY MINS. OF EXERCISE/ MEDITATION I DID :

DAILY REFLECTION:

HOW MANY HOURS OF SLEEP I GOT LAST NIGHT:

HOW MANY HOURS OF SLEEP I PLAN TO GET TONIGHT:

My Thoughts

IT'S TIME TO RELEASE THE PAST & LIVE IN THE PRESENT.

"I am becoming the best version of myself everyday"

Queen, sometimes we need a break. Plan a night away in a hotel or commit to planning a weekend getaway.

WHAT ARE YOU THANKFUL FOR?

Slayed the Day

TODAY, I'M GRATEFUL FOR: _____

WHAT I ATE TODAY:

Breakfast:
Snacks:
Lunch:
Dinner:

HOW MANY OZ. OF WATER I DRANK:

HOW MANY MINS. OF EXERCISE/ MEDITATION I DID :

DAILY REFLECTION:

HOW MANY HOURS OF SLEEP I GOT LAST NIGHT:

HOW MANY HOURS OF SLEEP I PLAN TO GET TONIGHT:

My Thoughts

KEEP EVOLVING AND ELEVATING.

My strength is greater than any struggle

Girl, surround yourself with love. Go to brunch with your best friends.

WHAT PEOPLE IN YOUR LIFE MAKE YOU FEEL LOVED AND APPRECIATED?

_____

_____

_____

_____

_____

_____

_____

Slayed the Day

TODAY, I'M GRATEFUL FOR: _____

WHAT I ATE TODAY:

Breakfast: _____

Snacks: _____

Lunch: _____

Dinner: _____

HOW MANY OZ. OF WATER I DRANK:

HOW MANY MINS. OF EXERCISE/ MEDITATION I DID :

DAILY REFLECTION:

HOW MANY HOURS OF SLEEP I GOT LAST NIGHT:

HOW MANY HOURS OF SLEEP I PLAN TO GET TONIGHT:

My Thoughts

SLOW DOWN & TRUST THE PROCESS.

"I refuse to be distracted from my goals and vision"

Girl, be a goaldigger!
Devote extra time to work towards
your goals today.

LIST SOME GOALS AND WHAT YOU NEED TO DO TO ACCOMPLISH THEM.

Slayed the Day

TODAY, I'M GRATEFUL FOR: _____

WHAT I ATE TODAY:

Breakfast:	
Snacks:	
Lunch:	
Dinner:	

HOW MANY OZ. OF WATER I DRANK:

HOW MANY MINS. OF EXERCISE/ MEDITATION I DID :

DAILY REFLECTION:

HOW MANY HOURS OF SLEEP I GOT LAST NIGHT:

HOW MANY HOURS OF SLEEP I PLAN TO GET TONIGHT:

My Thoughts

YOU CAN'T POUR FROM AN EMPTY CUP.

Sis, music can be therapeutic.
Make a playlist of your favorite songs
and just groove to it.

HOW WOULD YOU DESCRIBE YOURSELF, IN A LOVING WAY, TO A STRANGER?

_____

_____

_____

_____

_____

_____

_____

_____

Slayed the Day

TODAY, I'M GRATEFUL FOR: _____

WHAT I ATE TODAY:

Breakfast:
Snacks:
Lunch:
Dinner:

HOW MANY OZ. OF WATER I DRANK:

HOW MANY MINS. OF EXERCISE/ MEDITATION I DID :

DAILY REFLECTION:

HOW MANY HOURS OF SLEEP I GOT LAST NIGHT:

HOW MANY HOURS OF SLEEP I PLAN TO GET TONIGHT:

My Thoughts

DON'T RUSH. WHAT'S FOR YOU IS FOR YOU.

"I will not settle for less than I deserve"

It's ok to treat yo'self, Babe!
Buy yourself something that you
really want.

WHAT GOOD HABIT DO YOU WANT TO BEGIN? COMMIT TO A DATE TO START DOING IT.

_____

_____

_____

_____

_____

_____

_____

_____

Slayed the Day

TODAY, I'M GRATEFUL FOR: _____

WHAT I ATE TODAY:

Breakfast:	
Snacks:	
Lunch:	
Dinner:	

HOW MANY OZ. OF WATER I DRANK:

HOW MANY MINS. OF EXERCISE/ MEDITATION I DID :

DAILY REFLECTION:

HOW MANY HOURS OF SLEEP I GOT LAST NIGHT:

HOW MANY HOURS OF SLEEP I PLAN TO GET TONIGHT:

My Thoughts

SPEAK WHAT YOU WANT INTO EXISTENCE.

"I am enough, no proof required"

Queen, stay hydrated!
Commit to drinking only water for one whole day.

WHAT IS THE BIGGEST STRUGGLE WITH FULLY LOVING YOURSELF?

Slayed the Day

TODAY, I'M GRATEFUL FOR: _____

WHAT I ATE TODAY:

Breakfast: _____

Snacks: _____

Lunch: _____

Dinner: _____

HOW MANY OZ. OF WATER I DRANK:

HOW MANY MINS. OF EXERCISE/ MEDITATION I DID :

DAILY REFLECTION:

_____

_____

_____

HOW MANY HOURS OF SLEEP I GOT LAST NIGHT:

HOW MANY HOURS OF SLEEP I PLAN TO GET TONIGHT:

My Thoughts

DON'T LET YOUR DREAMS EXPIRE.

"I know my value and worth"

Girl, unwind and have a little fun.
Go to happy hour with your friends.

HOW CAN YOU START STEPPING OUT OF YOUR COMFORT ZONE?

_____

_____

_____

_____

_____

_____

_____

_____

Slayed the Day

TODAY, I'M GRATEFUL FOR: _____

WHAT I ATE TODAY:

Breakfast: _____
Snacks: _____
Lunch: _____
Dinner: _____

HOW MANY OZ. OF WATER I DRANK:

HOW MANY MINS. OF EXERCISE/ MEDITATION I DID :

DAILY REFLECTION:

HOW MANY HOURS OF SLEEP I GOT LAST NIGHT:

HOW MANY HOURS OF SLEEP I PLAN TO GET TONIGHT:

My Thoughts

IT'S OK TO NOT BE OK.

"*I am responsible for my happiness*"

Sis, healthy skin is in!
Pamper yourself with a relaxing facial
or start a skin care routine.

WHAT ARE YOU AFRAID OF? HOW CAN YOU OVERCOME THAT FEAR?

_____

_____

_____

_____

_____

_____

_____

_____

Slayed the Day

TODAY, I'M GRATEFUL FOR: _____

WHAT I ATE TODAY:

Breakfast: _____

Snacks: _____

Lunch: _____

Dinner: _____

HOW MANY OZ. OF WATER I DRANK:

HOW MANY MINS. OF EXERCISE/ MEDITATION I DID :

DAILY REFLECTION:

_____

_____

_____

HOW MANY HOURS OF SLEEP I GOT LAST NIGHT:

HOW MANY HOURS OF SLEEP I PLAN TO GET TONIGHT:

My Thoughts

DO NOT SETTLE FOR LESS THAN YOU DESERVE.

Babe, refresh your environment. Add some newness or redecorate a space in your home or office.

ARE YOU HOLDING ANY GRUDGES? IS IT TIME TO FORGIVE SOMEONE WHO HAS WRONGED YOU?

_____

_____

_____

_____

_____

_____

_____

_____

Slayed the Day

TODAY, I'M GRATEFUL FOR: _____

WHAT I ATE TODAY:

Breakfast:
Snacks:
Lunch:
Dinner:

HOW MANY OZ. OF WATER I DRANK:

HOW MANY MINS. OF EXERCISE/ MEDITATION I DID :

DAILY REFLECTION:

HOW MANY HOURS OF SLEEP I GOT LAST NIGHT:

HOW MANY HOURS OF SLEEP I PLAN TO GET TONIGHT:

My Thoughts

DON'T COMPARE YOURSELF. YOU ARE EXACTLY WHERE YOU NEED TO BE.

Sis, it will be ok, just breathe.
Engage in some deep breathing
exercises.

WHAT MOTIVATES OR INSPIRES YOU?

_____

_____

_____

_____

_____

_____

_____

_____

Slayed the Day

TODAY, I'M GRATEFUL FOR: _____

WHAT I ATE TODAY:

Breakfast:
Snacks:
Lunch:
Dinner:

HOW MANY OZ. OF WATER I DRANK:

HOW MANY MINS. OF EXERCISE/ MEDITATION I DID :

DAILY REFLECTION:

HOW MANY HOURS OF SLEEP I GOT LAST NIGHT:

HOW MANY HOURS OF SLEEP I PLAN TO GET TONIGHT:

My Thoughts

YOU CAN OVERCOME ANY OBSTACLE THAT COMES YOUR WAY.

Girl, feed your mind.
Listen or watch an inspirational
podcast or video.

HOW WILL YOU COMMIT TO LOVING YOURSELF MORE?

_____

_____

_____

_____

_____

_____

_____

_____

Slayed the Day

TODAY, I'M GRATEFUL FOR: _____

WHAT I ATE TODAY:

Breakfast:	
Snacks:	
Lunch:	
Dinner:	

HOW MANY OZ. OF WATER I DRANK:

HOW MANY MINS. OF EXERCISE/ MEDITATION I DID :

DAILY REFLECTION:

HOW MANY HOURS OF SLEEP I GOT LAST NIGHT:

HOW MANY HOURS OF SLEEP I PLAN TO GET TONIGHT:

My Thoughts

REMEMBER, SELF-CARE ISN'T SELFISH.

My Thoughts

My Thoughts

My Thoughts

My Thoughts

My Thoughts

My Thoughts

My Thoughts

My Thoughts

My Thoughts

My Thoughts

My Thoughts

My Thoughts

My Thoughts

My Thoughts

My Thoughts

Made in the USA
Las Vegas, NV
24 January 2024

84864720R00079